Cardinal
★ FEVER ★

Go Cards

J. TERRY JOHNSON

Cardinal
★ FEVER ★

Cardinal Fever

Editing by Kylie Lyons
Cover and Interior design by Kandi Evans

Published in the United States of America

ISBN: 978-1-60799-769-6

1.Juvenile/ Youth/ Sports Memoir
09.05.04

DEDICATION

This book is dedicated to my seven grandchildren—Tanner Clark, Tyler Clark, Travis Clark, Josh Brown, Ashley Brown, Emily Brown, and Mitch Brown—whose lives are full of wonder as they transform themselves from children into adults. May they retain the joys of their youth, always able to recapture the innocence and purity of their childhood years. And may one or all of them take up the torch of being a St. Louis Cardinal fan.

ACKNOWLEDGMENTS

What I have observed over the past six decades is that avid fans of any athletic team are developed over a period of many years. Those who introduce the initiate to a certain team, its legends, and folklore are merely passing the baton to a new generation of fanatics. Consequently, having the "fever" is a *result* of one's becoming a fan; it is never the *cause.*

I will always be grateful for my father and mother, who supported me and my passion for baseball. A special word of thanks is also extended to Mr. Kelly and Dick Shadwell, who stirred the juices of my imagination and nurtured my exploding fascination with the St. Louis

Cardinals baseball team. The seeds they sowed years ago continue to bear much fruit.

Mr. Michael Glenn, local history librarian at the Springfield Greene County Public Library, was most helpful in my acquiring permission to use some of the photographs of the Frisco trains and of the passenger stations in Springfield and St. Louis, Missouri. I especially want to thank Louis Griesemer and the Springfield Underground, Inc., for allowing me to use these photographs and for Mr. Griesemer's sharing his valuable collection of Frisco photographs and memorabilia with the public.

Once again, the team at Tate Publishing has been at my side throughout the editing, layout, and graphic design phases of publishing this book. I offer a tip of my Cardinal cap to Kylie Lyons for her editing skills and to Kandi Evans for her graphic design and layout concepts. Both women are professionally gifted and pleasant to work with as colleagues.

I am honored that Whitey Herzog, a legend of the game, consented to write the foreword to *Cardinal Fever.* If anyone knows the value of loyal fans, it is Whitey. He led the Cardinals throughout the 1980s, winning three National League championships (1982, 1985, and 1987) and the World Series in 1982. Those were unforgettable years for Cardinal fans. We all have a warm spot in our hearts for Whitey and for what he accomplished as the team's manager.

Finally, I want to express my admiration for the work being done at the Missouri Sports Hall of Fame in Springfield, Missouri. To Jerald Andrews and Marty Willadsen, who currently lead that program, and to all of those who support the Hall with their financial resources, I say thank you. I pledge to contribute a part of the royalties of *Cardinal Fever* to support the ongoing work of the Missouri Sports Hall of Fame.

CONTENTS

Whitey Herzog

FOREWORD

Baseball fans come in all shapes and sizes. Male and female. Young and old. Those who reside in palatial mansions and those who make their homes in the tenements. What they share is their love for a game affectionately known as America's pastime.

During my years in the Major Leagues, I always appreciated the fans. Without them, the success we enjoyed on the field would have been hollow victory. Their enthusiastic participation in the grandstands provided my team and me the added incentive we needed to play the game at the highest possible level.

Some cities are known to be baseball towns. St. Louis is one of those communities. The fans that support the Cardinals have always been recognized as some of the most loyal and knowledgeable in the game. Over the past century, the St. Louis fans and the team have celebrated many pennant winners and ten World Series championships.

Terry Johnson has captured some of the magical moments of a young kid growing up in "Cardinal country." He taps into the everyday experiences that contribute to the development of a genuine baseball fan.

Written primarily for youth, *Cardinal Fever* is a delightful read for adults as well. I especially enjoyed the nostalgic trip back into the late 1940s and early 1950s when Stan Musial and Red Schoendienst were the Redbird stars.

Steal a few minutes to read this book. Then share it with a friend, a child, or a grandchild. *Cardinal Fever* is a tribute to you—the American baseball fan.

—Whitey Herzog

THE WONDER OF IT ALL

The stifling summer air blanketed downtown St. Louis. A hazy blue sky was cloudless, and the flags lay still, absent even a trace of wind. The last rays of sunshine on a scorching July afternoon shimmered on the huge arch looming over the "Gateway City." This was what I had been hoping for—*a perfect night for baseball.*

A near-sellout crowd gathered outside Busch Stadium, home of the St. Louis Cardinals. They came by bus, by rail, and in car caravans from cities and farm towns in Missouri and many neighboring states—families, for the most part, just like Mitch and I. All of us were covered in red to show support for the home team.

I was wearing my favorite red and blue Cardinal cap,

sporting the logo of a redbird perched upon a yellow bat. Mitch was dressed in his red Mark McGwire shirt—CARDINALS written across the front, and McGwire's number, 25, displayed prominently on the back. This wide-eyed six-year-old was big time into "Big Mac."

Mitch was making his inaugural trip to St. Louis. Every landmark we visited was an opportunity for me to recount stories from years past. At the top of our day's agenda were Forest Park, Union Station, and the mighty Mississippi River, with its armada of excursion boats plying the muddy waters, separating Illinois and Missouri. All of this had been thrilling to share, but nothing had me more excited than accompanying Mitch to a baseball game of my beloved Cardinals.

"Mitch, do you have a Major League Baseball cap?" I asked. Vendors were everywhere, working the crowd to peddle their logo wear and souvenirs.

"I've got a blue one at home," he replied.

"Does it have a 'T' on it?" I asked, well aware that his dad was a long-time Texas Rangers fan.

"Yes, sir," he answered, using his best West Texas manners.

"Well, let's see if we can get you a red one tonight," I said. "When you're with Papa, we go all out to show our support for the Cardinals."

We saw some caps at a small souvenir stand near the

stadium. They competed for display space with pennants and jerseys and a host of stuffed animals, all dressed in Cardinal red. A wiry, blond-headed teenage boy appeared to be in charge. As we approached, he was making small talk with a pack of gangly boys his own age. Before we could attract his attention, my patience began to run thin.

"Excuse me," I said as politely as I could manage, trying to get the boy's attention. "We want to see one of your Cardinal caps in a boy's size." Although I knew Mitch was a growing boy and would fare well having an adjustable cap, I wanted him to have a real baseball cap.

"Got any regular wool caps made especially for boys?" I asked.

"Not for a kid his size," he said, eyeing Mitch with some skepticism that he actually needed a fitted cap. "Check the team store inside the stadium," he offered before turning his attention back to his friends.

Mitch and I moved on, knowing there would be plenty of souvenir stands ahead.

Near our entry gate, we saw the larger-than-life bronze statue of Stan "The Man" Musial in his "peekaboo" batting stance.

"Do you know who this is?" I asked.

"No, sir, not really," Mitch replied.

"Stan Musial was the greatest player to wear the

St. Louis uniform," I said proudly. "No one else comes close to holding as many Cardinal batting records as he does."

"Was he better than Mark McGwire?" Mitch asked, unbelieving that anyone could rival "Big Mac."

"By a long shot," I answered. "He didn't hit as many home runs as McGwire, but you can be sure he was a better overall player. And Stan Musial was a great leader on and off the field."

I gave Mitch a brief baseball history lesson on the slugger from Donora, Pennsylvania. Musial had been my childhood hero. My loyalty to the Cardinals was due, in large measure, to his staggering athletic achievements over a span of twenty years.

A silver-haired gentleman and his wife were admiring the bronze likeness of the legend. With my camera extended toward the onlookers, I asked, "Would you mind taking a photo of my grandson and me?"

Mitch and I splashed goofy grins on our faces, blinked as the flash went off, then thanked the man and continued our trek in search of an entrance.

Growing up in Southwest Missouri, I had been infected with "Cardinal fever" before I began the first grade. For years my wife and two daughters had put up with my passion for baseball, worrying about a grown man unable to detach from his childhood fantasies. At night I sat for hours listening to the faint and garbled broadcasts of Cardinal games over a car radio because it was the only place I could get any reception.

But now I had a new audience—young ears that had not yet heard the names Slaughter, Schoendienst, Gibson, or Musial, nor had they listened to Harry Caray or Jack Buck broadcast the play-by-play. A youthful mind that knew nothing of Sportsman's Park or the "Gas House Gang." All of that was about to change.

I handed two tickets to the man at the turnstile, and we moved into the dark walkways below the stadium. There the familiar smell of spilt beer and hotdogs simmering on a greasy grill stirred a sense of nostalgia, reassuring me that I was back in the bowels of Busch Stadium.

"Get your programs, scorecards, souvenir yearbooks here!" bellowed a hefty redheaded man teetering on top of a tall stool.

"We need a scorecard and one of your yearbooks," I said, searching my pockets for stray dollar bills.

Gone were the days when scorecards could be purchased for a dime. Today's version was made of colorful card stock plastered with advertising and cost seventy-five cents. And the souvenir yearbooks? Six dollars! But it was money well spent—a small price to pay for a fledgling Cardinal fan on the cusp of fanaticism.

Mitch and I made a beeline to the team store where "fan-wear" came in every size, shade, and style. We found a red Cardinal cap in a boy's size. It was a bit large for Mitch's round little head, but it was the real McCoy—not one of those ugly wannabe adjustable caps. What kind of baseball player would ever wear a cap with a hole in the back?

"*Now* you look like a Cardinal fan," I said, a smile breaking across my face as pride welled inside. "No one will think twice about the team you're rooting for tonight. C'mon, let's check out our seats." I wanted Mitch to share my excitement of seeing the players on the field.

We climbed the ramped walkways, moving past one vendor after another, and found our section.

"Here we go, Mitch," I said. "We go right through this opening and then we'll find our seats."

Perfect, I thought to myself as we surveyed the field. Groundskeepers were putting the final touches on white chalk-marked baselines, the organist was playing "happy music," and broadcasters were interviewing some of the players in anticipation of tonight's contest.

Our seats were in line with third base, ten rows behind the visitors' dugout. It was no accident that we were seated on the third-base side of the field. This was the same section where I had seen my first Major League game more than fifty years ago—a different stadium but the same area of the grandstands. Being a creature of habit, I often returned to that familiar territory when selecting my seats.

Mitch was awestruck by the panorama that lay before him. His eyes darted from the pitchers running sprints in the outfield to the batting cage where line drives were being launched in every direction. It was more than he could absorb in one viewing.

"Mitch, this is a great place to catch foul balls, so keep your glove handy," I teased.

I hoped the thought of catching a souvenir baseball might keep him focused on the action taking place on the field. In all my years of attending Major League Baseball games, I had never come close to catching, or chasing down, a foul ball; but, then, you never know. When a ball goes into the stands, someone goes home with the prize…and tonight that someone *could* be us. Mitch pounded his fist into his mitt as if to say, "*I'm ready.*"

From the moment we sat down, Mitch soon grew impatient watching the players take their batting and fielding practice. He moved the seat lid up and down a dozen times and laughed at "Fredbird," the Cardinal mascot. What brought him the most excitement were the vendors ambling down our aisle, hawking their overpriced popcorn, cotton candy, peanuts, hotdogs, and cold sodas. My billfold was open for all who came our way.

"Look, Mitch!" I said. "There's Mark McGwire, number 25, over by first base."

McGwire, who had hit a record-breaking seventy home runs the year before, was the most famous Cardinal on the field. Mitch had a large poster of "Big Mac" hanging on his bedroom wall. Now, there he was, taking some easy warm-up throws from the other infielders.

"When will we get to see him bat?" Mitch asked. That was a fair question. We hadn't come all the way to St. Louis to see Mark McGwire take infield practice; we wanted to see him hit one out of the park.

"The game is about to begin," I assured Mitch. "McGwire will be at bat before you can say 'Jackie Robinson.'"

"Who's Jackie Robinson?" Mitch asked, a hint of curiosity in his voice.

"Stand up for the National Anthem," I said, rising to my feet and placing my cap over my heart, "and I'll tell you all about Jackie Robinson some other time."

The ball game did not go our way. The New York Mets established an early lead and never let the Cardinals back into the game. McGwire went hitless in four times at bat, knocking only one ball out of the infield.

The outcome of the game appeared to make little, if any difference to Mitch. He took it all in stride, showing no emotion about the home team's loss. But I knew that before long my love for the Cardinals would rub off on him, and he'd soon be begging Papa to take him on another trip to St. Louis. And this time, we wouldn't settle for anything less than a Cardinal victory.

While Mitch and I joined the disappointed fans leaving Busch Stadium, I thought about my own love for the game and where it all began...

Downtown St. Louis as seen from the Gateway Arch

The goldfish pond on South Jefferson

WHERE IT BEGAN

Fifty years ago, Springfield, Missouri, was an All-American City. The "Queen City of the Ozarks" was what the local Chamber of Commerce liked to call it. I called it *home.*

Life was good in Springfield. Dazzling redbud and flowering dogwood trees competed each spring to put on the more stunning display of color. The maple trees transformed the fall months into a photographer's wonderland. The gentle roll of the Ozark Mountain foothills allowed free-flowing rivers to spill into scenic lakes.

"What more could anyone ask?" my dad was fond of saying. As far as he was concerned, Greene County, Missouri, was the center of the universe.

Our home was a two-bedroom framed house on Jefferson Street, located fifteen blocks south of the city's bustling downtown square. No one ever confused the neighborhood for the affluent part of town, but homeowners took pride in their modest homes and maintained their flower beds and front yards. Had Ozzie and Harriet Nelson lived in Springfield, they would have been right at home on Jefferson Street.

My grandparents were the original owners of the one-acre lot and had built the house and its detached garage twenty years before I was born. Now they made their home in a much larger two-story house near Phelps Grove Park.

Although our house was small, the lot ran deep. The sprawling acre was full of tall trees to climb, secluded places to hide, and wide-open spaces for a kid to play. Each spring Dad marked off a section on the back side of the property, plowed up the rocky soil, and planted a garden. We ate fresh fruit and vegetables from the garden all summer long, and Mom canned enough to feed our family well into the early winter months.

Until my brother, Tim, was born, I had lived in the lower-middle-class neighborhood for almost six years as the only child in our family. There were a few other children who lived on the block, but much of my free time was spent creating games that I could play alone. One day I was Roy Rogers, King of the Cowboys, and the next day I was G. I. Joe. Imagination was my best friend.

Our neighbors to the south were the Kellys. Mrs. Kelly was seldom seen, but her husband was often outdoors, working on his lawn or tending his small garden. He had a first name, but I never knew what it was; to me, he was Mr. Kelly.

"Mr. Kelly saved your life when you were just a toddler," my mom would occasionally remind me.

One morning I became a little too curious about the goldfish darting around our pond and slipped into the lily-covered attraction. Had Mr. Kelly not been outside, I might not have been able to pull myself from the slippery hole in the ground.

One thing I remember well about our neighbor is that Mr. Kelly owned the best-looking dog I had ever seen. She was a collie named "Lassie," just like the high-spirited, heroic dog I had seen at the movie theater.

"Hi, Mr. Kelly," I said one crisp fall afternoon as he was raking leaves in his front yard. "Where's Lassie?"

"She's getting groomed for the movie," he said.

"What movie?" I asked. Mom hadn't said anything about Lassie's being in a movie. This was exciting news.

"Well, there's a Hollywood film crew coming to Springfield to shoot a movie," he said without cracking a smile. "They want to use our dog to play the real Lassie.

"They're looking for a young boy to play a special part in the movie," Mr. Kelly went on to say, baiting me. "I think you would be perfect for the role, but they want someone who is especially quick on the draw with a pistol."

For weeks I wore my cap gun tucked into its holster on a huge Western-style belt that was cinched tightly around my waist. In view of our neighbors' windows, I practiced my "draw," much to Mr. Kelly's amusement.

Mr. Kelly's Lassie

Mr. Kelly was a big St. Louis Cardinal baseball fan. Almost every evening during the summer months he sat on his front porch and listened to the staticky broadcast of the game featuring the familiar "voice of the Cardinals"—Harry Caray.

None of us had a television in those days, but who needed one when Harry Caray gave us the play-by-play account of the game. No fan loved the Cardinals more than Harry.

"There she goes!" Harry would shout. "Way, way back there. It might be…It could be…It is, a home run. Holy cow!" When Harry was at his best, no one was better in the broadcast booth at a baseball game.

Over the course of the season, Mr. Kelly helped me develop an interest in a game I grew to love and for a team that stole my heart forever. Night after night we rooted for the Redbirds—an aging Cardinal fan and his five-year-old neighbor. We were the original "odd couple."

"Who're they playin' tonight, Mr. Kelly?" I asked one evening.

"Brooklyn," he replied in a hushed voice, so as not to miss a word from Harry or Harry's sidekick, Gabby Street. "The Bums are leading, three to one. It's the bottom of the third, and the Cards've got the bases loaded."

"Who's up?" I asked, brimming with excitement that we might score a few more runs.

"Rice," he replied. Del Rice was the Cardinals' light-hitting catcher that year—solid behind the plate but not especially gifted with the bat in his hands. "He's in a terrible slump." Mr. Kelly sighed, giving up on the poor guy before he had a chance to take a swing at the ball.

In a flash I tore across Mr. Kelly's driveway and into my front yard, up the porch steps, and into my house. When I returned, panting for breath, I was wearing my St. Louis Cardinal gray flannel shirt.

A small iron-on patch with a single redbird perched on a bat adorned the front of the jersey, and Mom had sewn a red 6 onto the back. My cap was blue with a red bill and had the familiar "S-T-L" lettering on the front. I carried a black baseball bat and my new Nocona first baseman's mitt.

"Too late," Mr. Kelly said, sadness lacing his voice. "Rice just struck out."

One of my make-believe games was to reenact the radio broadcast play-by-play in my front yard. Mr. Kelly would let me know who was at bat, whether he had swung and missed, had taken a pitch, or had driven the ball deep into the bleachers, and I would act out the scene. Two ground-level tree stumps and a huge maple tree were first, second, and third bases, and the front porch steps of our house served as home plate.

The highlight of every game was when Stan "The Man" Musial, who wore the real number 6, was up to bat. Mr. Kelly taught me what it meant to bat left-handed and how to ape the famous Musial crouch. Stan Musial was the most admired baseball player in the whole wide world. He was a young boy's perfect model on and off the field. I knew that was true because Harry Caray had said so many times.

Every story must have its beginning. My romance with baseball began there in that front yard on Jefferson Street—a five-year-old kid with a Cards cap, an old radio, and a mentor who nurtured my love for America's great pastime. It spread to the sandlots of Sunshine Elementary School and then to the Kiwanis League summer youth baseball program. Throughout all of those years, even today, I have been a St. Louis Cardinal fan. Sometimes I find myself whispering almost reverently, "Thanks, Mr. Kelly, wherever you are."

Springfield Depot, circa 1947

DAD AND THE DEPOT

My dad worked over thirty years for the Railway Express Agency. REA, as it was commonly known at that time, was in the business of moving all kinds of freight. Most of it was sent across the country by rail. Dad's job was a backbreaker, requiring him to load heavy crates in and out of boxcars that passed through the Springfield Depot. His hours were long and often extended from late at night into the early hours of the morning.

Each train depot—whether large or small—had its own REA office. The head agent of the local office managed the operations, supervising a staff of clerks and truck drivers. Dad had worked only a couple of years with REA before he shipped out with the United States Army for a two-and-a-half-year tour of duty during World War II. He fought with the allied troops in the Philippines and in New Guinea. When he returned home in 1945, his job with REA was waiting for him.

Since Dad didn't have many years of working experience, he drew the short straw in picking his shift and days off, meaning he had to work nights, sleep days, and spend time at the depot on weekends. To make matters worse, he returned from the war with a back injury that gave him grief the rest of his life. Sometime, while lifting a heavy piece of freight, his back would go out on him. When this happened, he would be laid up in bed, suffering unbearable pain for days.

"You'll have to play outside today," Mom would inform me, "but don't make too much noise near your dad's window because he's sleeping. His back is hurting again."

I knew that meant I needed to spend some time down the block with the neighborhood kids. It was best that I be at their house playing baseball rather than them coming over to mine. Things were going to be shut down at home for a while.

Our family owned only one car—a 1941 beige Dodge coupe that Mom's brother had given to us when Dad came home from the war. On the days when Mom didn't need a car, Dad would drive the Dodge to work and leave it in the depot parking lot. More often than not, Mom needed wheels for her errands, so she would drive my dad to work and then pick him up nine or ten hours later when his shift was over.

I always liked it when Mom sent me inside the depot to find Dad and let him know we were there to take him home.

"Go find your dad and tell him to hurry. We're going on a picnic tonight," Mom said as she reached across my lap and opened the car's passenger door. Her tone was direct but reassuring that I could take care of her request.

And off I went, out of the car and into the REA offices, looking for Dad.

An endless sea of tan cardboard boxes and wooden crates, the place smelled stuffy like a glue factory. Most of the freight was of no interest to me. Many of the boxes were identical to the ones stacked beside them.

What was fun, however, was finding the animals that were being shipped that day: sometimes a dog, maybe some chickens, and, every now and then, rabbits or white mice being sent to a scientific laboratory. I searched for all the animals as if I were on a treasure hunt.

Everybody at the depot knew my dad. He was good-natured and cared about people. Folks liked him, and wherever he went, laughter, teasing, and good humor usually followed. Although his first name was Clifford, his fellow workers called him "Johnny," which seemed odd to me because no one else used that name to address my dad. I always wanted my friends at school to call me Johnny too, but it never quite caught on.

If everything was going as planned, Dad would be in the office filling out his daily reports; however, I would usually find him somewhere in the freight warehouse or outside on the tracks, loading or unloading one of the boxcars. Two or three trains could be serviced at any given time, and if one happened to be running late, it threw everyone's workday into a tailspin.

"Hey there! You looking for Johnny?" Clyde Justice, one of Dad's fellow workers and a good friend, asked.

I knew Mr. Justice better than most of the REA employees. He lived around the corner from our house, and his family went to the same church we did.

"Yes, sir," I said. "Mom's waiting outside."

"He's working the number four train that came in late from St. Louis," Mr. Justice said. "He should be back soon. You can probably find him just outside and down the tracks to your left."

The telephone rang, and Mr. Justice paused to answer. I waited just long enough to give him a wave and then scooted down the stairs, through the freight room, and out the north doors that led to the tracks.

The trains were the main attraction at the depot. It made no difference that they were outdated and loud and soon to be overshadowed by airplanes. The old steam engines still chugged their way through most routes, but when a new diesel engine roared into town, all eyes were on its arrival.

The passenger trains were the superstars: the *Texas Bluebonnet,* the *Texas Special,* the *Meteor.* As I passed by these Goliaths of the steel tracks, I kept my distance, for one could never be certain when one of them might let off a little steam—literally.

Having spotted Dad hauling some boxes and crates back to the depot, I waved to get his attention.

"Mom said to hurry!" I yelled, straining my voice to be heard over the deafening roar of a switch engine creeping by on a nearby track.

Dad sat upon a noisy mule—not an animal, mind you, but a tractor he used to transfer the inbound freight from the boxcars to the REA warehouse. It emitted a strong metallic odor, reminiscent of diesel fuel and burnt oil.

"We're going to the park tonight," I said in a loud voice.

He smiled and told me to hop on one of the wagons he was pulling behind the mule.

"It'll be at least another thirty minutes before I can

get my reports turned in," Dad said, wiping beads of sweat from his forehead. "Ask your mother if she wants to wait or come back later."

That very scene played out many times in my early years. There was nothing fancy about my dad's job or where he worked; there were, however, plenty of interesting things to see for a curious young boy who enjoyed being around trains. From one day to the next, I never knew what surprise might be in store for me when I visited the depot.

Frisco diesel engine – 1947

THE METEOR

"Where are we going for lunch?" I asked Mom one Sunday morning after attending church services. My stomach growled like a bear.

"We're going to meet your dad for lunch at the Harvey House," Mom replied. She knew I would be thrilled with the news.

Sometimes when Dad was working on Sunday, he would ask Mom and me to meet him at the Harvey House Restaurant, which was located in the train terminal next to the main passenger waiting room. The REA office, where Dad spent his weekends processing paperwork, was on the other end of the depot.

"What sounds good today?" Dad asked as he and Mom looked over the menus.

"I want fried chicken," I answered, almost before he finished his question. He already knew my order because it was the same every time we ate at the Harvey House. The aroma of skillet-fried chicken filled the dining hall and was a teaser I could never pass up.

"Your passes for the train trip to St. Louis came in today," Dad announced as we waited for our lunch to be served.

"Finally," Mom said. "I was beginning to worry about them. We leave next week."

Railroad employees, including those who worked for the REA, were entitled to a limited number of free train passes each year. In prior years Mom and I had used the passes to see my aunt and uncle in Dallas, but this was my first trip to St. Louis.

"Are we going to see the Cardinals? You promised, Mom," I pleaded.

"We'll see," she answered. "We may not know for sure until we get there."

"You'll be riding on the *Meteor,*" Dad said. "It's got one of the new diesel engines."

The *Meteor* always arrived in Springfield during the wee morning hours. The evening before our trip, I laid out my clothes for the next day and hopped in bed much earlier than my normal bedtime hour. Mom and Dad had set an alarm clock for 3:00 a.m. so they could arise early and get me up just in time for our drive to the depot.

"Hey, sleepyhead," Dad said, tickling my feet. "Time to rise and shine. The train will be here soon."

It didn't take long for me to get my bearings. On any other day I might have grumbled and pulled the pillow over my head, falling back to sleep, but not this morning. This was the day I had been waiting for all summer, and I wasn't going to miss a minute of it.

Because there were few cars on the streets at such an early hour, the trip to the depot took only a few minutes. Dad parked the car and began unloading our suitcases and carry-on items. I was in a hurry to get inside.

Mom and Dad had a brief visit with the agent at the ticket window, confirming our passes were in good order. We checked in our larger pieces of luggage and then waited in the station's main lobby for the *Meteor* to arrive. If lucky, it would be on time, but, more than likely, it would be running anywhere from a half-hour to two hours late.

The massive wooden benches were not intended to be very comfortable. Mom said the stationmaster didn't want people to lie down and go to sleep, and the iron armrests made that almost impossible. I squirmed and fidgeted in my seat until I heard a familiar, welcome sound.

"This is the first call announcing the arrival of the *Meteor,*" a booming voice proclaimed over the depot's primitive public address system. "Boarding for St. Louis will begin in approximately five minutes on track number one."

"Is that our train, Dad?" I asked excitedly.

"This is the one," he answered. "And she's only twenty minutes behind schedule this morning. You should be in St. Louis by nine thirty, no later than ten."

We walked from the lobby, through the doors, and down the wide platform that lay next to the tracks. There we waited for the first glimpse of the engine's probing light.

"Here she comes!" I squealed.

At first the train did not look impressive. It appeared small in the distance, and its whistle whined rather faintly in the cool morning air. But as she approached the station, the mammoth size of the diesel engine became an awesome sight. I backed away from the tracks and found myself clutching my dad's big hand, my heart racing as the train made its approach. Silently, I counted the cars as they passed—six, seven, eight, nine—ten cars in all.

With brakes screeching and one final blast of billowing steam, the *Meteor* came to a jerky stop almost five hundred yards beyond where most of us were standing. Our family followed alongside other boarding passengers who moved quickly in the direction of the waiting coach cars. Since our luggage had been checked at the depot, all we needed were our passes and, of course, any snacks that we might wish to eat along the way.

The first member of the train's crew to hit the ground was usually the brakeman, followed closely by the porter, and then the conductor. The porter placed a large, moveable step just below the stairs that led up into the front or rear passageway of a coach car.

It took several minutes for the Springfield-bound passengers to deboard the train, making their way down the steps and moving on toward the depot. A few of them were hardly awake. They didn't appear nearly as excited to be leaving the train as I was to be boarding it.

"All aboard," the conductor sang as he moved up the steps of the idling train and then disappeared from our sight.

Mom and I said our good-byes to Dad—a hug, a kiss, and a wave of the hand—and it was up the steps and into the coach car reserved for St. Louis-bound passengers.

Coach cars were equipped with rows of cushioned chairs, mostly facing forward, but with a few facing the rear. I preferred a window seat with a rear view—something you just couldn't get while riding in most automobiles. We stowed our carry-on items in the overhead nets and settled in for the four-and-a-half-hour ride.

It was not always easy to tell when the train began to move. Sometimes it would jerk or make a grinding noise that would signal we were rolling, but more often than not, the initial movement was hardly noticeable. At night, without many visible reference points to be seen out the windows, it was even more difficult to know for sure that the train was in motion. Within minutes, however, as steel wheels began to move over joints in the steel rails, the *clickety-clack* gave us a good feeling that our trip was finally underway.

The first hour on the *Meteor* was uneventful. It was dark outside, and the scenery was nothing but a black blur. As we passed by some small towns, there were streetlights, some porch lights, and a few flashing red lights at sleepy intersections. Soon the porter came by, offering pillows, followed by the conductor, who examined our passes.

"Where are you going, young man?" the conductor asked, his voice deep and smooth.

"Mom and I are going to St. Louis," I answered proudly.

He seemed pleasant enough but never made much eye contact. His focus was on his job, looking at the passes or tickets handed to him and then poking holes in them with his handheld punch. He attached a paper stub on a clip high above the window next to our seats, indicating that we were paid up until St. Louis but no farther.

As he was about to move on, he asked, "Plan to see the Cardinals play while you're in St. Louis?"

"Yes, sir, I think we are," I answered, more assuredly than I had reason to believe. "How did you know?"

"Well, I just had a hunch when I saw your Cardinal cap," he answered. "When Marty Marion comes to the plate, cheer extra loud for me. I'm a big fan of 'Slats.'" Marion was the lanky, smooth-fielding shortstop for the Redbirds known more for his glove than his bat.

"I will," I said excitedly, and he moved on.

Soon streams of daylight began to break in the east. It became much easier to see what we had been missing as the *Meteor* passed through the small Missouri towns.

Since we were hopefully going to attend a ball game sometime during the week, I looked to see if there were any clouds in the sky. Nothing could ruin a long-awaited trip to St. Louis more than a ball game postponed because of rain. From what I could see, it was going to be a beautiful, sunny day.

"Are you ready for breakfast?" Mom asked. I nodded my head vigorously, as I was always ready for breakfast.

The diner was one of the more interesting cars on the train. The food was overpriced, but it was fun to eat any meal at a place that had linen-covered tables, fancy dishes, and polished silverware. Waiters swayed gracefully to the rhythm of the moving train while balancing trays in their open palms, held high above their heads.

Breakfast served on the *Meteor's* dining car

Breakfast on the train was not always so much about the food as it was about the "show." Mom sipped her morning coffee, watching me gulp down my orange juice, milk, pancakes loaded with maple syrup, and a side of crisp bacon.

"Someone was hungry this morning," our waiter said. "Was it good?"

"The pancakes were all right, but I like my mom's better," I said, bringing a smile to Mom's face.

After we had been aboard the train four hours, we began to see the outskirts of St. Louis. The *Meteor* had slowed down and was moving at a crawl past row houses, school playgrounds, and junky warehouses. More automobile traffic was stacked up at the railroad crossings as we rumbled past the blinking lights. Each passing scene merged into the next.

"This is Webster Groves," Mom said. "Let's get everything we brought with us. We'll be at Union Station in just a few more minutes."

Looking out the windows on either side, I could see nothing but trains and tracks. Freight trains were everywhere, and two other passenger trains were either on their way in to the docking platforms or on their way out. Our engineer had moved the *Meteor* past Union Station, brought it to a halt, and slowly backed us into the berth that had been reserved for our arrival.

With help from the porter, Mom and I stepped off the train and walked toward the terminal to claim our luggage. Union Station was everything the Springfield Depot was not—it was huge, it was impressive, and it was as busy as a firecracker stand on the Fourth of July. At one time in its fabled past, Union Station had been recognized for being the "busiest railroad terminal in the world."

Mom made sure I noticed the enormous vaulted ceiling, along with the stained glass and mosaics that graced the huge windows and walls. No doubt about it, St. Louis had a great train depot. Union Station made a very good first impression on a young kid who was already in awe of the big city.

Interior of Union Station, St. Louis, Missouri

MEET ME IN ST. LOUIS

It was a short taxi ride from Union Station to the apartment where Mom and I would be staying while in St. Louis. The seven-story building was two blocks from Grand Avenue on West Pine, near St. Louis University, the oldest university west of the Mississippi River. Our host was a kind woman with an unusual name: Alameda Fritz. Until then I had never met anyone named Alameda, nor have I since.

Alameda was old enough to be my grandmother, but she had never married. She had spent her entire working career with the Railway Express Agency. Most of that time, she was secretary for some of the top officials in the St. Louis office. She was loyal to her faith, to her country, to her fellow workers at the office, and to the St. Louis

Cardinals, but I couldn't say for sure it was always in that order.

During the war, Alameda had written letters of support to those soldiers, and their families, who were on military leave from the Express Company's St. Louis district, including those who had been working in the Springfield office. While Dad was in the war zones of New Guinea and the Philippines, he had received several letters from Alameda. She told him what was happening in Missouri, especially news about the REA. Alameda also sent letters during those difficult months to Mom in Springfield. From that time on she was considered a very special friend of our family.

Alameda's residence was a small one-bedroom apartment located on the third floor. A rickety, old elevator was her way of getting to her unit. There were stairs, of course, but she never used them. The elevator was not much more than a metal crate that shook all over as it crawled up and down the open shaft.

"Where's the operator?" I asked.

Every elevator I had seen had an operator. At the department stores the operators wore uniforms and greeted you as you stepped inside the car. "Floor, please?" they would ask as they pulled one handle to close the door and another to send the car up or down. Their job was to see that the passengers got safely to their requested floor.

"This elevator is self-service," Alameda said. "Do you want to push the button?"

Looking quickly at Mom, who nodded in approval, I pushed hard on button number three. The elevator shook for a few seconds and then began its slow ascent to the third floor. When we stopped, Alameda pulled on the door handle, and we stepped out into a hallway. A few doors down the hall we found unit 305.

Alameda was the only person I had ever known who lived in an apartment. The furniture was squeezed in, with everything tucked into its own tiny space. But what really blew me away was the Murphy bed that pulled out of her living room wall.

"Have you ever slept in a bed like this one?" Alameda asked. I shook my head.

It frightened me to think that I could go to sleep in the bed tonight, and at any minute it might spring back into the wall. To my surprise, Mom and I slept like logs on the pull-down contraption. It was much more comfortable than I had imagined.

Having no car of her own, Alameda used public transportation to get wherever she needed to go. Each morning she rode the streetcar to work and returned home the same way. If she needed to go somewhere that wasn't within easy walking distance of the streetcar or bus line, she would call a taxi. Alameda certainly knew her way around the city.

St. Louis happened to be one of the few Midwestern cities that enjoyed a rich Catholic tradition. Mom said it had something to do with the city's early French settlers who brought their religious practices with them centuries before our time. Having had no other religious experience than attending Sunday school and church services with Mom and Dad, I had never encountered many people who had a faith that was much different from my own.

It surprised me to learn that Alameda was Catholic, and a devoted one at that. Our family didn't know very many Catholics back in Springfield, so the idea of being with someone who spoke kindly about the Pope was quite new to me.

On Sunday morning, Mom and I attended mass with Alameda. The cathedral was huge, much larger than the church building where we worshipped at home. And it was dark, almost spooky, causing me some angst as I held firmly to my mother's hand.

The worship service was different from anything I had ever experienced. The priests were all in fancy robes, speaking in a language I did not understand. There were rows and rows of candles and lots of fragrant smoke that made me want to sneeze.

"Mom, is that a fire?" I asked with some concern in my voice.

"*Shh,*" she scolded. "That's incense. We'll talk about it later."

There were so many things I had never seen before in a worship assembly—lots of kneeling and readings from a prayer book, men in robes strolling up and down the aisles, and a huge organ playing hymns that were never sung at our church services back home. Being so young, I made no judgments as to whether these changes were good or bad they were just different.

Like almost everyone in St. Louis, Alameda was a Cardinal fan. She knew that I was one too.

"Who's your favorite player?" she asked, already knowing the answer.

"Stan Musial," I said. Who else could she have possibly had in mind?

"I hope he hits a homer for us Tuesday night," she said, making sure I knew we were going to see the Cardinals in person. It would be my first Major League Baseball game.

"He hit two against the Pirates the other night," she continued, "and I'll bet he has some more where those came from." I was tantalized, and excitement mounted just thinking about a dream so soon to come true.

Monday was a workday for Alameda, so Mom and I caught a bus that took us to Forest Park, home of St. Louis's famous zoo. We had a zoo in Springfield, but it was a postage stamp compared to Forest Park's sprawling grounds. We saw many unusual animals I had never seen before. There were apes and giraffes and bears of all colors and sizes, pacing in their open-air pens. And I saw exotic lizards and poisonous snakes crawling on rocks and trees inside their glass cages. It was a feast for a young boy's eyes.

"We need to hurry," Mom said, "or we might miss the monkey show."

"Monkey show?" I asked, my curiosity piqued. "What's that all about?"

"Come on," she said. "You'll see."

The Forest Park Zoo had three amazing animal shows. The chimpanzees were dressed up like people and did funny tricks. The elephants paraded around in a circle and then stood on two legs on small stands. The lion tamers cracked their whips, directing the lions and tigers, which scared the pants off me. Those shows were almost as good as watching the famous Barnum and Bailey's Circus.

Later that evening Alameda joined Mom and me for another visit to Forest Park—this time to attend a show at the Muny Opera. The Muny was a theater under the stars, featuring special stage shows that were touring throughout the States. *Showboat* was playing, and it was my first time to hear the beautiful lyrics and music of "Old Man River." I had never heard anyone sing with such a rich, deep voice.

Alameda took a day off work on Tuesday and joined Mom and me for a shopping trip to downtown St. Louis. Mom had promised to buy me some new school clothes to start the second grade. Once again, we used the streetcar, catching it on Grand Avenue and making the transfer that took us to the center of the city.

The only thing I ever found ugly about St. Louis was the soot and grime that marred the appearance of the downtown buildings. The black soot was everywhere—the result of a time when businesses relied mostly on coal for heat in cold weather. At that time the city officials had expended little effort to clean up the damage caused by the smokestack industries.

The downtown department stores were enormous. One store filled an entire city block. The three of us spent the first twenty minutes window-shopping. We strolled along the outside of the buildings, looking at the colorful displays of new fall clothes.

"Let me shop a few minutes for some items on my own list, and then we'll find the boy's department for your school clothes," Mom said. "You'll need some shirts and jeans, maybe some socks and a jacket."

"Can I get a new baseball bat too?" I asked.

"That's not on my school clothes list," Mom answered, her tone warning that I was skating on thin ice.

The stores had such unusual names: Famous Barr, Styx, Baer and Fuller. I thought it strange that St. Louis didn't have a Heer's, which was Springfield's largest department store. But, truthfully, I preferred the St. Louis stores. They had many mind-boggling items that Heer's didn't have.

This was especially true in the sports department. The St. Louis stores had so many more Cardinal souvenirs, Cardinal emblems, and Cardinal photos. They even had a baseball bat my size with Enos Slaughter's name on it.

"Mom, can we get it?" I begged. "It's just what I've always wanted."

"We'll see," she said, smiling. "You have a birthday coming up in a couple of months. Maybe we can do something about it then."

After having lunch in the tearoom, I found another thing those department stores had that we didn't have in Springfield—puppet shows to entertain children. *Hansel and Gretel* was performed that afternoon, and I had a front-row seat.

The show was tons of fun, and I wanted to stay and see it again, but it was time to go back to Alameda's apartment.

"We need to get ready to see the Cardinal ball game tonight," Mom reminded me.

For sure, I thought. That's what our whole trip was all about—attending my first Major League Baseball game!

Sportsman's Park, circa 1950

SPORTSMAN'S PARK

Sportsman's Park was home field to both the St. Louis Cardinals and to their lesser-known cousins of the American League, the St. Louis Browns. Only once had both teams made it to the World Series in the same year. It was 1944 when the Cardinals whipped the Brownies four games to two. Since there were two teams and only one stadium, one team was on the road while the other was playing in St. Louis.

In the 1940s there was no other Major League team located west or south of St. Louis. These two clubs, especially the Cardinals, had a large group of fans throughout the Midwest and much of the Southwest. Radio broadcasts were beamed to distant states and provided fans with play-by-play accounts of the games.

The Cardinal players became famous in many areas west of the Mississippi River, and the team itself was very successful. Four times in the past eight years the Cardinals had won the National League pennant—1942, 1943, 1944, and 1946—and they had gone on to win the World Series each of those years except 1943. That year they lost to the New York Yankees four games to one. Tonight was my night to see what the "real deal" was all about.

Alameda had purchased tickets from an employee benefit program at her office. The evening at the ballpark had been her idea, and it was her treat. From that day on she and I were very good friends.

Getting to the ballpark could not have been easier. The three of us walked the two blocks from the apartment on Pine Street to its intersection with Grand Avenue. There we caught the streetcar that took us all the way to Sportsman's Park.

Almost all of the riders on that streetcar were going to the game. Once we stepped on board, we were immersed in a sea of Cardinal red. The mood was loud, even rowdy at times, but it was fun. After all, everyone was rooting for the Redbirds.

"Did you see that play at the plate last night?" a young man asked the gentleman seated next to him. "There is no way they could have called Country out."

I knew the play they were talking about because

Alameda had read the article to me from the morning newspaper. Enos "Country" Slaughter had tried to repeat his famous run in the 1946 World Series against the Boston Red Sox. In that game he went from first base all the way home on a double to left field. This time, however, he had been called out on a close play at home plate, costing the Cardinals a much-needed run.

"Who are the Giants throwin' tonight?" the young man continued.

"Jansen," the gentleman replied. "He's been their best pitcher all year. It should be a great game."

That's what I wanted to hear. You bet it was going to be a great game. I was getting more and more excited with each *clang* of the streetcar's noisy bell.

★★★★

The old ballpark at Grand and Dodier was not very attractive, nor was it very clean, but to a six-year-old kid from the Ozarks, it was an unbelievable sight.

Large steel pillars blocked some of the view for those unfortunate fans who were seated behind them. Alameda had done us right, however; our seats were well in front of those pillars. We had a great view of the field from the third-base side of the grandstands. My eyes were as big as baseballs as I tried to take in the whole scene at once.

Looking out over the playing field, I was surprised there was so much to see. The bases were much farther apart than those stumps in my front yard. And dugouts—I didn't know that teams were seated in dugouts! There was so much more color and commotion going on throughout the ballpark than I had ever been able to imagine while listening to the radio.

The field was bustling with activity, and I hardly knew where to look. Behind the bleachers in left field was a huge scoreboard that was operated by hand. It presented the line score of our ball game along with the scores of other Major League teams that were playing in faraway cities.

The players were dressed in their very best flannels. For the first time I realized that the home team always wore white uniforms and the visiting team wore gray.

"Do the Cardinals ever wear gray uniforms like the Giants?" I asked Alameda.

"Sure they do," she replied. "Whenever they play on the road, they wear their gray uniforms. It's been that way for a long time."

Taking nothing away from the Giants, but the Cardinals certainly won the fashion show that night. Their white jerseys and bloomer-style pants were trimmed with Cardinal red. Two redbirds perched upon a bat were spread across the chest of each player. Their socks were red with white stripes, and their caps were just like the one I had brought to wear at the game.

The sportswriters and radio broadcast teams had special boxes high above home plate. Most of them wrote for the newspapers and wire services. There were a few radio announcers and Western Union teletype operators sending the scores all across the nation. My granddad worked for Western Union in Springfield and had told me lots of stories about his covering high-profile ball games. I could imagine what it must have been like for him to sit in one of those press boxes.

Alameda made sure I saw where the legendary Harry Caray was seated.

"Look over to your right," Alameda said. "Harry is the one who has the fishing net sticking out of his booth."

How many times had Mr. Kelly and I heard Harry and Gabby talk about a foul ball coming toward them and one of them reaching for the net? And there they were—Harry Caray and Gabby Street—the voices of the St. Louis Cardinals.

Harry didn't look anything like I thought he would. He wore large eyeglasses and had wavy, almost curly hair. From where I sat he looked more like a helper for Buffalo Bob on *The Howdy Doody Show* than he did a radio broadcaster. He certainly didn't look like the person whose voice I remembered hearing at Mr. Kelly's house.

Finally the Cardinals ran out from their dugout and

onto the field. It was time for the game to begin! We all stood for the National Anthem, and then the home plate umpire motioned for the teams to "play ball."

Howie Pollet was pitching for the Cardinals. He was thought to be St. Louis's best hurler. Pollet had helped the Redbirds win the pennant four times in recent years. The first three batters he faced went down easily. I felt sure that was a good sign of things to come.

As the innings moved along, I noticed that Alameda was making some funny-looking marks on her scorecard. She knew how to take shorthand at her office, and she also knew how to score a baseball game. I showed just enough curiosity for her to teach me how to keep score too. Once I knew how to number the nine positions on the field, it was fun.

We had skipped dinner so we could eat at the ballpark, and my stomach soon reminded me that it was time to eat. Vendors were busy working the crowd all night long.

As was true of most kids my age, I loved hotdogs. In fact, I had eaten more than my share of hotdogs at cookouts in my own backyard. But the one I ate that night at Sportsman's Park was the best I had ever tasted—anywhere. Since that night I have learned that no visit to a baseball game is complete without eating at least one "red-hot." Spread mustard all over it and see if you can down it in three bites—well, maybe four.

The game drifted along into the middle innings with no score. Howie Pollet and Larry Jansen were hooked up in a classic pitchers' duel. But in the bottom of the sixth, Marty Marion drove in the game's only run with a single to right field. I knew the train conductor would be happy. Pollet held the Giants the rest of the way, and the Cardinals came away with a 1–0 victory.

"You mean it's over?" I asked in disbelief. "Aren't they going to play any more?"

"Nine innings." Alameda smiled. "Nine innings is all they play, unless the score is tied. Then they play more."

Everything had happened so fast. Too fast! I was happy that we had won, but I wanted more. It was like having a big thirst that had not yet been fully satisfied.

★★★★

That evening's game was the first of many trips I have made to St. Louis to see the Cardinals play baseball. Some games have been more exciting, but there can never be another game like the "first." I couldn't wait to get home and share every detail with Dad and Mr. Kelly.

Silver Eagles, Springfield Kiwanis League, 1952

DWARFS, SILVER EAGLES, AND MIDGETS

It's one game to swing a bat at a make-believe ball, thrown by an invisible pitcher, then circle the tree stumps in your front yard. It's a whole different ball game to play real baseball as a member of a team.

The first time I can recall playing baseball with kids my age was at recess on the Sunshine Elementary School playground. Of course, it really wasn't baseball; it was softball, but I hardly knew the difference.

Not many of the first-grade boys played softball. They preferred to chase the girls or play tag. I liked to chase the girls too, but I always kept one eye on the older guys who were playing ball on the other side of the playground.

One day the second-graders needed an extra player to complete their team. I asked if I could fill the spot.

"You can play right field and you will be last to bat," said the second-grade team captain.

That didn't matter to me. I was just glad to be able to swing the bat, throw the ball, and run the bases. I loved the game!

By the time I began the second grade, our class could make up two teams at recess if we joined with the third-graders and allowed a few of the girls to play. Two players were chosen to be captains, and they selected their own squads.

"I choose David," said the first captain to select a player. David Trotter could hit the ball a mile. Everyone wanted him on their team.

"Let me have Kenneth," said the second captain. Kenneth Sharp was as fast as the wind. He couldn't hit the ball as far as David, but he could circle the bases faster than anyone else on the ball field.

Although usually selected within the first three picks, I had to swallow hard a few times when Linda Blinn was chosen before my name was called. She could really wallop the ball.

The Kiwanis Club of Springfield sponsored the summer league baseball program. Most players on a team came from a local school or the same quadrant of the city. There were a few recruits from distant neighborhoods, but unlike our school playgrounds, no girls were invited to play in the Kiwanis League.

Each age level, from seven to fourteen, made up its own division. First- and second-place trophies were given to members of the championship teams. Games for the younger boys were played on the softball fields at the city parks.

Times and places for each week's games were published in the local Sunday newspaper. As you might expect, many of the teams used "Cardinals" in their name. There were the Mac Cardinals, the Doling Cardinals, the Willard Cardinals, and the Delaware Cardinals, just to name a few.

For reasons I never understood, my first Kiwanis League team was called the "Dwarfs"—not the Tigers, not the Wildcats, but the Dwarfs. Who was going to fear a team named the Dwarfs? We had a psychological disadvantage before we took one step onto the field.

Our uniform consisted of gray pants with scarlet-red trim down the sides. We wore red socks and a red cap with a white block-letter "D" on the front. Our shirts were the same as every other team in the program: a white tee shirt with the Kiwanis International logo printed on the front. It was the first time I had ever worn a real baseball uniform.

"You look like a ballplayer," Mom said as she straightened my cap. "Now go out there and get a home run today."

"Thanks, Mom," I said. "But I'm not sure I'll even get to play today."

Hitting a hardball thrown overhanded by someone other than a friendly coach was difficult for me. I was one or two years younger than most of the boys who played for the Dwarfs. A good day at the plate for me was to be walked. A really good day was to be walked twice!

"Don't swing until you have two strikes," Coach Hawkins would say to me as I came to the batter's box. "If you walk, we will have the top of the lineup to drive you home."

I knew he didn't believe I could hit the ball. His doubts made me wonder if I could hit it either.

My defensive play wasn't much better. When not sitting on the bench, I spent a few innings in right field. Coach Hawkins never dreamed of placing me in the infield. I was a little discouraged by the whole idea of playing team baseball. It would have been easy for me to give it all up.

Somewhere in the middle of the second season with the Dwarfs, I began to make contact with the baseball.

At times it was nothing more than a weak ground ball back to the pitcher or maybe a pop fly to the first baseman. But on a few occasions, I ripped the ball past the infielders and into the outfield. My confidence began to soar. There were no heroic moments, but the game became fun once again.

In my third summer of Kiwanis ball, I played for a team made up of boys more my own age. We were the Silver Eagles—a far more fitting name for a baseball team. That year the caps were blue with a white "S" and "E" on the front. Instead of real baseball pants, however, we wore blue jeans. Judging only by our "uniforms," it would have been easy to miscalculate the talent we had on the team.

Our coach, John Challender, was a building contractor whose son played shortstop. Coach didn't smile very much, but he knew a lot about baseball. He made us practice almost every day that we weren't scheduled to play a league game.

"You're going to be my second baseman," Coach told me one afternoon just before practice. "Just get down with the ball and always keep it in front of you."

Then he began to hit grounders to all of us who played the infield. I booted a few, smothered a few, and, every now and then, fielded the ball cleanly. Making the throw to first base was always an adventure, but by the end of the season, second base was my position.

Led by our star left-handed pitcher, Steve Lunsford, the Silver Eagles had a very successful season. The team finished second in the league, losing the championship game by a single run. In addition to Kiwanis League games, we traveled to nearby towns, playing other teams in our age bracket.

At the end of the season, Coach Challender hosted an awards banquet where he presented us with our second-place trophies and made some remarks about the team as a whole.

"This team has been better than I thought it would be," Coach began. "You have more talent than you realize."

Then came the shocker. Coach asked me to come forward and receive a silver-plated bracelet for being the Silver Eagles' "most valuable player." For a couple of years I wore the bracelet as a symbol of personal achievement. Knowing that someone else thought I was good at the game made me want more of the same experience.

After one more year with the Silver Eagles, I caught a break. As our season was came to a close, Carl Arnold, coach for the Berry Midgets, asked me to play for his team the next year. The Midgets were one of the best teams in our league.

"Son, I've been watching you play ball this summer," Mr. Arnold said. "What about playing for the Midgets next year?"

Oh, great! I thought to myself. *I have already spent two years as a Dwarf, and now I'm being asked to play for a team named the Midgets.*

But then he sweetened the offer.

"We have a new sponsor for next year—Newberry's Five and Dime Store on the square," Mr. Arnold said. "They're supplying us with new uniforms, including matching jerseys for our out-of-town games. And they're also providing enough money for the team to have new bats and balls."

Mr. Arnold had planned games well into the fall with teams from small towns near Springfield. I decided to travel with the Midgets, playing baseball all over Southwest Missouri until cold weather finally settled in. Our parents drove us to our games and cheered us on to many victories.

We traveled to Branson one night, Reeds Springs the next, and on to Lebanon the week after that. Maybe it was the boost in my confidence, but I tore the cover off the ball that fall game after game. Baseball was beginning to claim a sizeable place in my heart.

That next summer the Newberry Midgets were the talk of the Kiwanis League. We beat the defending champions in the final game of the playoffs and won the handsome first-place trophies. Even my brother, Tim, who served as our team's batboy, received a trophy for his efforts. For several years those little statuettes were in our bedrooms as a reminder of our championship season.

One of the lessons I learned that year was, championships come at a cost. Mr. Arnold believed in practice. We made it through the trial of playing or practicing baseball day after day in 100-degree weather. Sweat mixed with dust from the field made mud on our practice uniforms.

"You must have worked hard today," Mom would say as I came into the kitchen following a practice session. "You're as dirty as I have ever seen you."

I began to understand that my mom thought my success on the baseball field was directly related to the amount of dirt I had on my uniform.

As a reward for the successful season, our parents took the team on a trip to St. Louis to see the Cardinals. We couldn't have been happier if we had been invited to meet with President Eisenhower at the White House. The Redbirds routed Cincinnati, 11–4. It was the perfect ending to a wonderful season.

THE MIGHTY YANKEES

Mom and Dad had many friends who enjoyed having picnics. Sometimes they met in each other's backyards or at one of the local parks. On special occasions they would cook out on gravel bars next to James River.

There was always plenty to eat—fried chicken, corn on the cob, baked beans—I liked it all. But my favorite food was anything that looked like dessert, especially homemade ice cream.

The parks were neat places to have picnics. The kids played shuffleboard or had fun on the slide and swing sets. If invited, I threw horseshoes with the men. On most evenings someone would get a game of softball going. That's what I liked best.

Among my parents' dearest friends were Dick and Gertrude Shadwell. Dick, who was known to his friends as "Shad," was always talking about sports. He was a great golfer and a big Cardinal baseball fan. He knew how much I liked the Cardinals, so we always talked about baseball whenever we saw each other at church or at one of the picnics.

"Say, did you hear that game last night?" Shad would say with excitement in his voice and a twinkle in his eye. "Isn't that Musial an unbelievable player? I believe he could hit an aspirin shot out of a B-B gun." Of course, he knew I agreed.

"Are you planning a trip to St. Louis this year?" I asked.

Shad worked for the Frisco Railroad and was also able to get free passes on the train. Once, when Gertrude was unable to make a trip to St. Louis, he had taken me to see the Cardinals play. I was always hoping for another chance to go with him.

"You know what I've been thinking?" Shad said, lowering his voice as if to see who might be listening to our little chat. "The Yankees are coming to St. Louis in August. I think it might be a good time to see them play the Browns."

The Yankees always drew big crowds wherever they played on the road. There were fans that loved the world-famous team from New York and even more who hated them. Their success brought them great fame and plenty of scorn.

"The Browns!" I stammered. It really surprised me that Shad would go to St. Louis to see the Browns. "Why would you waste your time watching those losers?" I asked in disbelief.

The poor Browns were almost always in last place, and I didn't care anything about the American League. I did watch some of the best players from the American League at the annual All-Star game in July, but I never rooted for them to win. The same held true of the World Series in October. Even if I had to cheer for Brooklyn, I wanted the National League team to win.

"Well," Shad said, "this may be the last year we get to see the Yankees in our part of the country. The Browns may not be playing in St. Louis much longer. From what I hear, they may be moving to another city.

"Besides," he continued, "the Yankees are loaded with talent this year. I'd love to see the new kid, Mantle, play center field. He may be better than DiMaggio."

Any baseball fan in our part of the country had heard about Mickey Mantle. He could hit home runs when hitting right-handed or left-handed. The slugger had grown up in Commerce, Oklahoma, just about a hundred miles southwest of Springfield.

Mantle had speed, power, and played the outfield as if he owned the place. With plenty of personality, he was also a favorite subject of baseball sportswriters and broadcasters.

The Yankees never seemed to lack for talented players. Babe Ruth, Lou Gehrig, and Joe DiMaggio were all gone. They had been superstars in their day. Now, the Bronx Bombers had even more star players—Yogi Berra, Phil Rizzuto, Hank Bauer, Allie Reynolds, and southpaw Ed Lopat. Add Mantle and they were as feared a team as any in Major League Baseball. And, as if that weren't enough star power, Casey Stengel, a first-class wiseacre, was their popular manager.

Then Shad asked the question, "Do you think you can talk your dad into getting you a train pass and go with me?"

Now I would rather he'd ask me to go with him to see the Cardinals, but a trip to St. Louis was always exciting. I told him I would work on it.

On the way home from the park, I broached the subject with my dad.

"Shad asked if I could go with him to St. Louis to see the Browns this summer," I began. "What do you think, Dad? Can I go?"

"Why would you want to see the Browns?" Dad

replied. I knew that was coming. He felt the same way I did about watching the hapless Browns.

"They're playing the Yankees, and I really want to see Mickey Mantle," I said, pleading my case. "Can I go, Dad? Please!"

Dad got the pass, and we marked the date on our calendar. The Browns played a four-game series against the Yankees in early August. The last two games were a doubleheader on a Sunday afternoon. Shad bought tickets for us to see those two games.

"This way we'll get twice as much baseball for the same ticket price," Shad said.

Shad and I got to the ballpark early that day. We wanted to be in our seats when the Yankees took their batting practice.

"Watching these guys hit is almost as good as the game itself," Shad said. "The Yankees are the best team in both the American and the National League."

"Which one is Mickey Mantle?" I asked.

"He's number seven," Shad replied. "Look just behind the batting cage. He may be next to hit."

Dressed in their gray road uniforms, the Yanks put on a show for us. They hit towering fly balls that cleared the outfield fences by thirty or forty feet. Those of us in the grandstands weren't the only ones watching. Several players for the Browns stood in front of their own dugout, hardly believing the Yankees could hit the ball so far.

Since the Browns played at Sportsman's Park, the same stadium where I had already seen a few Cardinal games, I was beginning to feel fairly comfortable walking around the stadium on my own.

"Shad," I asked, "would it be all right if I went downstairs to see if I can get a few autographs?"

"Sure," he answered with some caution in his voice, "but be back in time for the start of the game."

Prior to each game the players from both teams had to get from their own dressing rooms to the baseball field. They went down some steps and across a walkway beneath the third-base grandstand. Then they had to go through the home team's dugout before going onto the field. Along the way they had to pass by a group of kids my age, and several adults, all begging for autographs.

"Did you get any good ones?" Shad asked as I returned to my seat.

"Ned Garver from the Browns and Johnny Sain from the Yankees," I replied with a big smile. "Phil Rizzuto stopped for a minute, but I couldn't get to him in time."

The afternoon went as we had expected. The Yankees won both games, 6–4 and 6–1. Mantle and Berra were the hitting stars, smashing home runs over the right-field pavilion, just as they had done in batting practice. Allie Reynolds and Vic Raschi got the pitching wins. No one from the Browns stood out in defeat.

Well, no one, that is, except the famous African-American pitcher, Satchel Paige. He pitched a couple of innings in relief during the second game. Prior to his coming into the game, Paige had been sitting in the Browns' bullpen along the third baseline, parked under a large umbrella. He had been watching the younger players working hard on the field. The Yanks got a couple of hits off Paige but could not increase their lead.

Paige, now in his fifties, had become known as a power-ball pitcher in the old Negro Leagues. He was among the first African-Americans signed to a contract by a Major League team. Jackie Robinson, who played for the Brooklyn Dodgers, was the first. His example made some big changes for the game, and Paige was one among many players who got to be in the Major Leagues because of what Robinson had dared to accomplish.

Unfortunately for Paige, his chance to play big league ball had come after his best years were over. He was more of a fan pleaser than anything special as a pitcher. But he was in uniform, striking out the Yankee batters with his "stuff."

That was the first and last time I ever saw the Browns play baseball. They may have been from St. Louis, but to me they were just another team—and not a very good one at that. The next time I came to Sportsman's Park, it would not be to see teams from the American League. I only wanted to see the Cardinals.

Autographed copy of Ted Williams postcard, circa 1953

BASEBALL CARDS AND AUTOGRAPHS

How a young boy becomes a baseball fan is an interesting study. Many things go into the process that leads him from his first swing of the bat to someone calling him a rabid fan. My own path would be similar to many others who have fallen head over heels in love with a Major League team.

As I have already said, radio broadcasts played a big role in my becoming a Cardinal fan. Harry Caray was a great salesman for the Cardinals. So was his fellow Baseball Hall-of-Fame successor, Jack Buck. Their styles were very different, but the influence each had over an audience was huge. Both were good for the game.

Long after my normal bedtime hour, I often listened to Cardinal games on my radio. The volume was always turned down low enough so that Mom and Dad would not be able to hear.

If the Cardinals were about to lose a lead in the late innings, I couldn't bear to listen. It was like watching a scary movie. I might turn the broadcast off for a few minutes, hoping Lindy McDaniel would strike out the side and get us out of the jam before I turned the radio back on. If Stan Musial hit a "walk-off" home run in the bottom of the ninth, I had to work hard not to yell, "Way to go, Stan!"

Daily newspapers and monthly sports magazines helped me maintain my love for baseball. The paperboy threw our paper onto the driveway each afternoon around 5:00. Every evening I tore into the sports section of the *Springfield Leader and Press* to see where the Redbirds were in the standings.

In the early 1950s there were only eight teams in the National League, and they were not separated into divisions. St. Louis would usually be ahead of Chicago, Pittsburgh, Philadelphia, Boston, and Cincinnati, but a few games behind Brooklyn and New York. I took it personally every time they moved up or down the ladder.

After reading the box scores, I would see if Stan Musial was still leading the league in hitting. Then I would check to see if any other Cardinals might be among the league leaders in hitting or pitching. If there were any photographs suitable for my Cardinals' scrapbook, I would carefully cut them out and paste them onto an empty page. These were not casual acts of devotion, but rather a daily routine.

"Mom, can I get a subscription to *Sport* magazine?" I asked one day.

"How much does it cost?" she replied.

"I don't know, but Doug gets it at his house," I said, certain that if my teammate on the Newberry Midgets could have it sent to his house, I could too.

"We'll see," Mom said. That's what moms always say whenever they don't want to disappoint you.

The next Christmas a subscription gift card was in my stocking. *Sport* and similar publications provided me with enough pictures to start another scrapbook of Cardinal stars. I read everything I could find that featured the Redbirds and soon knew all about their personal lives as well as their professional baseball careers.

But for a young boy in the 1950s, nothing defined his interest in baseball more than the size of his baseball card collection. The packets of bubblegum and cardboard photos were the toys for boys who had outgrown their tricycles and cap pistols. It had little, if anything, to do with the future value of the cards—although a few of these young traders, years later, sold their collections for thousands of dollars. It had everything to do with being a baseball fan.

A package of six cards cost a nickel, and that included a card-size piece of bubblegum. Two or three wads of Bazooka gum in his mouth would make any Little Leaguer look just like tobacco-chewing Nellie Fox. He was the star second baseman for the Chicago White Sox. I liked that look, so I always had plenty of gum with me when we played our Kiwanis League games.

I began collecting baseball cards in 1951 and had complete sets of the Topps series for several years in a row. Shoeboxes and metal file drawers were ideal for storing the cards. My closet was full of stuffed boxes, loaded with the current year's cards in numerical order, and duplicates sorted according to teams.

"Mom, Brad wants me to go with him over to the dime store to pick up some baseball cards," I said one afternoon, begging her to let me go along. "Can I ride my bike over there with him?"

Brad Lovell was a neighbor who was a couple of years older than I. We traded cards and used some of our duplicates to make an awful noise in our bicycle wheel spokes. Since he had a paper route, Brad always had a little more pocket change to buy cards than I did.

"Be home before supper," Mom would answer.

And off we would go, ready to purchase a few more cards. We always hoped each pack would include some Cardinal players, or at least some cards we didn't already have.

On rainy days when no one was playing baseball in the neighborhood, I would pull out my baseball cards and create my own all-star game. Each league would be represented by the best players in my collection. Using a plain deck of playing cards, I thought up a game that allowed each hitter in the lineup to take his turn at the plate. As I turned over a playing card, it told me whether he got a hit or made an out.

Cardinal cards were rarely used as "trade bait" for my collection. They were always special. But, occasionally, if I needed a card to complete a set, I might consider swapping one of the Redbirds to a friend.

"Bruce, do you have an extra 1952 Mantle?" I asked one of my friends. "I'll give you a Solly Hemus and a Ray Jablonski for it."

Bruce Hollowell was a pitching star in the Kiwanis League. Being one of the few pitchers my age who could throw a curve ball, he made all of us look foolish at the plate. Bruce was also known to have the largest collection of baseball cards in town.

"Not any extra ones, and if I did, it would take something pretty special to make a trade," Bruce replied. "A whole lot more than Hemus and Jablonski. Check with me next week and we'll see what we can work out."

In addition to the baseball cards and photo scrapbooks, I collected autographs and photographs directly from the players. Each trip to Sportsman's Park was my chance to add signatures for my autograph collection. Most of them were Cardinals, but a few gems came from the visiting teams: most notably, pitcher Warren Spahn of the Braves and Frank Robinson, star outfielder for the Cincinnati Reds. Two of my favorite autographs were from Cardinal broadcaster Harry Caray and National League umpire Augie Donatelli.

The photographs took time to collect, and the process was never a sure bet. Each spring I wrote directly to a few players on teams from all over the Major Leagues, asking for an autographed photo. Only a few responded. Some sent me a postcard-size photograph, while others sent 8x10-inch glossies. A few were personally signed, while others had a stamped signature.

"Mom, look what I got in the mail!" I yelled one morning.

"Come, show me," Mom said as she sat down at the kitchen table. "What have you got?"

"It's a photo postcard of Ted Williams, and it's personally autographed!" I gasped. "This one is really special."

Ted Williams was not my favorite player. He played for the wrong team. In my opinion, he also played in the wrong league. But he was one of the best players ever to wear a Major League uniform. The value of my collection got a big boost.

Mitch in Dodger blue

MIDLAND SANDLOT BALL

Four years had passed since Mitch and I enjoyed our grandfather-grandson outing at Busch Stadium. He was the oldest of four children, having two sisters and a little brother. From what I could observe, Mitch was always the leader among his siblings. Regardless of the situation, he was never happier than when he was in charge.

The only home Mitch had ever known was Midland, Texas. People who live elsewhere think of West Texas as the jumping-off spot of the world. The land is flat and dry, and the tallest trees are scrubby mesquites. In fact, on much of the land, you are more likely to discover giant oil wells instead of trees.

Everyone agrees, however, that it is the people from these cities that make West Texas a great place to live and raise a family. People who come from Midland, Texas, are best known for their friendliness, their independence, and their character. After all, people like President George W. Bush and First Lady Laura Bush got their starts in the friendly city on the West Texas plains.

Mitch, now in fourth grade, was head over heels into sports. He knew the stats of his favorite NBA players and had posters of professional athletes covering his bedroom walls. Albert Pujols, the sensational new Cardinal first baseman, had replaced Mark McGwire as his favorite Major League Baseball player, but Mitch was also into Dallas Cowboys football and Los Angeles Lakers basketball.

As did many boys his age, he collected baseball and football cards by the hundreds. Whenever he and his dad were not playing catch or tossing a football in the backyard, they were watching football, basketball, and baseball games on their big-screen television in the family room.

A year earlier, just as the World Series was about to begin, Mitch and his dad had accompanied both of his grandfathers on a trip to Cooperstown, New York. The beautiful village, home to Major League Baseball's Hall of Fame, is the visual opposite of West Texas. Majestic trees, rolling hills, and steel-blue lakes provide a picturesque setting for baseball's venerable shrine.

Every baseball fan needs to make that trip at least once in a lifetime. Ruth, Williams, Mays, Mantle, Musial, and so many more—they're all there—the exceptional superstars who grace the pages of baseball's storied past. You can be sure that I called Mitch's attention to every Cardinal photograph we could find—and there were plenty on display.

"Look over here, Mitch," I said as we entered into a new room. "This is a picture of the old Cardinal Gas House Gang. Look, here is Dizzy Dean with his brother, Paul."

"Did you see them play?" Mitch asked.

"Whoa," I sputtered. "That was a little before my time. But," I continued, "every Cardinal fan knows about that team. The Gas House Gang played a special brand of baseball."

Over the years I have been able to watch Mitch play in many different sporting events. He was a point guard on his basketball team, a defensive back on his Pop Warner football team, and one of the more aggressive players on his soccer squad. From the time he was eight he could par a hole from almost any 150-yard marker at the Midland Country Club's golf course. When it came to athletics, there wasn't much that Mitch wouldn't try.

One night, I was in Midland to watch Mitch and his Little League Baseball team. The Dodgers were scheduled to play the league-leading Braves in an early-evening game under the lights. There was Mitch, in Dodger blue. I would have to forgive him for that. It wasn't his fault that his team's coach happened to be a Dodgers fan.

Earlier that afternoon Mitch and I had gone to the batting cage to take a few swings. He had good form with the bat and made contact on almost every pitch. Having been coached not to swing too hard, however, Mitch appeared to be listless at the plate.

"Don't be afraid to take your cuts," I said. "Step into the ball and give it a rip."

I could only imagine what kind of player Mitch might become in another three or four years when he would get some better batting tips from more experienced coaches.

The game turned out to be a dandy. Batting second in the lineup, Mitch lined out to the second baseman in the bottom of the first inning. It was not one of those scorching line drives, but he hit the ball hard enough to cause the infielder to take off his glove and rub his hand when the play was over.

"That's all right, Mitch!" I yelled. "We'll get 'em next time."

No one scored the first four innings. Playing second base, Mitch made a good play of a ground ball hit to his left, throwing the runner out by no more than a step. He had poise on the field and kept his head in the game.

It was a special treat to watch a grandson play the game I had grown up loving. I was a proud papa, sitting in the bleachers behind home plate, but then I would have been proud of Mitch whether he ever played baseball or not.

In the bottom of the fifth inning, the Dodgers began to rally. After a walk to the eighth batter in the lineup, the ninth man reached first base on a throwing error by the shortstop. Two on and no one out.

The leadoff batter got the signal from his coach to bunt, and he laid down the perfect sacrifice, just inside the third baseline. The pitcher came off the mound like a cat but was unable to handle the ball. Now the bases were loaded, and Mitch was on his way to the plate. I could only hope that he wasn't feeling the same butterflies that were fluttering around in my stomach.

The first two pitches were low, into the dirt. The catcher made good blocks of both to keep the runner on third base from scoring.

"Make him pitch to you, Mitch!" I yelled.

Good baseball coaching would have been for Mitch to take a pitch until the pitcher could show that he could throw a strike. After all, two more balls and the Dodgers would have their first run of the game. But I wanted to see Mitch hit the ball—not walk. I hoped that the pitcher would find his control. And he did.

The next pitch was right down the middle of the plate, no more than waist high. I watched anxiously as Mitch lifted his left foot ever so gently and moved it toward the pitching mound. Then his aluminum bat came flying over home plate.

The sound of bat on ball was not the same *crack* I had been used to as a kid. We only knew about bats made of wood. Nonetheless, there was no mistaking the fact that the ball had been well struck.

I watched as the ball shot off Mitch's bat, rising rapidly over the second baseman's outstretched glove,and into the gap in right center field. The ball rolled all the way to the fence, allowing all three runners to score, leaving Mitch in a cloud of dust, safely hugging third base.

"Atta boy, Mitch!" I shouted. "That's the way to give it a rip." He stood a few inches taller than usual on third base, paying no attention to the crowd as he dusted off his uniform.

"That's my grandson," I proudly announced to the

small group of fans in the bleachers. From their response, I knew they had already made the connection.

By that time my pride was totally out of control. I hadn't yelled so loud and so long in years. Those three runs turned out to be the only ones the Dodgers would need, as they held on for a 3–1 victory and a share of first place.

Mitch was quiet about his game-winning hit, but I could tell he was pleased that I had seen him perform at his best. His teammates gave him high-fives and hearty whacks on the back. The whole family celebrated the win with ice-cream sundaes at Baskin Robbins. We spent the rest of the evening recalling the game's highlights one inning at a time.

Bronze of Stan Musial signing an autograph,
Missouri Sports Hall of Fame
Springfield, Missouri
Photo courtesy of Preston Dial Photography

STAN THE MAN

Over the next three years, my wife and I made many trips to visit our kids in Midland. Mitch continued to play a few team sports and worked hard on his golf game. During the baseball season, he and I shared stories about a few Major League teams and their players. In my heart, I hoped he was becoming a bigger fan of the Cardinals.

"Did you see that Pujols hit three home runs against the Pirates the other night?" I asked.

"Yes, sir, but the Cardinals still lost the game," he said. "They need to get more innings out of their starting pitchers." I couldn't argue with that. For the past month or more, their pitching had gone into the tank.

"What are your favorite teams this year?" I asked

Mitch, hoping to hear that the Redbirds were still high on his list.

"Well, the Cardinals are my favorite team, but I also really like the Yankees this year," he said with a big grin on his face. "They're my favorite American League team."

"If you like the Cardinals and the Yankees, you would have loved the 1964 World Series," I said, remembering the event as if it were yesterday.

"Mimi and I were married that year," I continued, "and we had just moved to Dallas. But for two happy weeks in October, all was right with the world. That was the year the Cardinals beat the Yankees in an exciting seven-game series. It was a Cardinal fan's fantasy."

"Papa," Mitch said, slightly changing the subject, "how old were you when you caught 'Cardinal fever?'"

Now that question took me a little off guard. I sure didn't want to drop the ball. Mitch had come a long way in his own interest in the Cardinals. The "fever" could be nipping at his heels.

"Mitch," I began, "do you recall seeing that big statue of Stan Musial in front of Busch Stadium?" I knew he did because the photograph taken of the two of us standing in front of it was on a shelf in his bedroom.

"Yes, sir," Mitch replied.

"Well, Stan Musial played a big role in my becoming

a Cardinal fanatic. Let's start with him," I said. And then I told him this story.

Among baseball fans there will forever be some question over "who was the greatest to play the game?" Babe Ruth's name is always mentioned. So is Ty Cobb's. Ted Williams, Joe DiMaggio, Rogers Hornsby, Willie Mays, and Henry Aaron are usually on the "short list." But truthfully, there is no way to answer that question. The most that anyone can do is to name those who are among the "best of the best."

That, of course, is what the National Baseball Hall of Fame at Cooperstown is all about. It has invited the legends of the game to send their caps and bats and gloves to their museum. Only the very top players are invited to be members of the Hall of Fame.

No one who has ever followed baseball would deny that Stanley Frank Musial earned his place in Cooperstown. He spent twenty-two seasons scaring the socks off the pitchers in the National League.

Musial was named Most Valuable Player in the National League three times. He won the league's batting title seven times. He was also named to the All-Star team twenty-four times (two All-Star games were played in some of those years). Three times he led St. Louis to World Series victories. He still holds most of the batting records for the Cardinals, forty years after he retired from the game.

Some Major League stars are known for living on the wild side of life, but not Musial. He was a gentleman on and off the field.

Today some baseball stars don't like to be thought of as "role models." Musial seemed to be comfortable with it. That's why kids looked up to him. I was one of those kids. Stan Musial was a big part of the buzz in my getting "Cardinal fever."

I was eleven years old, soon to be twelve, when my mother brought a baby boy home from the hospital. It was her third son. No girls. Just three boys, each born six years apart.

Expecting a girl, Mom and Dad had several names picked out, but none were for a boy. At once I began to beg them that my baby brother be named Stanley Frank and that we all call him "Stan."

"Mom, this is important," I said as I visited her in the St. John's Hospital one evening. "You know how much this means to me. Please name him Stan."

To my surprise, Mom and Dad chose to name my brother Stanley, but they selected Charles as the middle name in honor of an uncle who lived in Texas. That was fine with me. I now had a baby brother, and we all called him Stan.

The next summer Shad and I made a trip to St. Louis to see the Cardinals play the Milwaukee Braves. The old Boston Braves had moved to Milwaukee, just as the old St. Louis Browns had moved to Baltimore.

The Braves were loaded with talent that year. In addition to their strong pitching staff, they had one of the best young outfielders in the National League—Henry "Hank" Aaron. I had no way of knowing that one day he would break Babe Ruth's lifetime home run record. That afternoon, however, we saw him collect one of those record-shattering homers.

Shad and I arrived early at Busch Stadium, the new name for old Sportsman's Park. He wanted to watch batting practice, but I had something else on my mind. After locating our seats, I ran to the area under the grandstand where the players made their way onto the field.

An overhead ramp had recently been built to allow the players to move freely between the clubhouse and the playing field. Now they could reach the field without being crushed by autograph hounds. Nothing, however, kept the players from reaching over the railing to oblige the fans.

Several players, in fact, had already stopped and signed some autographs that day. I had picked up Warren Spahn's signature and a few others, but I was waiting for the "big guy"—number six! A few minutes later he appeared, making his way down the ramp.

Sadly, Musial was running late that day and had no time to stop for autographs. I had already thought that might happen, and I knew what I had to do. As he passed, I yelled at the top of my lungs, "Stan! Stan! I named my baby brother after you."

Musial stopped in his tracks and came back up the ramp. He reached down for my autograph book and signed the blank page. He didn't say a word, and he didn't take the time to sign any other books or scorecards. That didn't matter to me. I had seen my hero face-to-face and had his autograph to prove it.

"Mitch," I said, "I had always been a Cardinal fan, but from that moment on I had 'Cardinal fever.'"

Mitch listened quietly as I told the story of Stan Musial and the influence he had had on a kid from Southwest Missouri. He seemed to be thinking about it all. After a few seconds, he looked at me and said, "Papa, do you think my mom and dad would let us change my brother's name from Josh to Albert?"

We shared a big laugh, but that's when I knew I had him. He was drinking the Kool-aid and was on the edge of becoming punch drunk with a good case of "Cardinal fever."

EPILOGUE

My most disappointing day in Busch Stadium was in 1987 during the National League Championship playoffs. The Cardinals were hosting the San Francisco Giants. The whole day was a disaster.

For starters, it was a very cold afternoon in early October. The north wind was blowing through the stadium, chilling all of us to the bone.

To make matters worse, our tickets were standing-room only. Whatever parts of our bodies were not numbed by the wind were aching from having to stand so long.

If that weren't bad enough, Giants lefty Dave Dravecky pitched a strong two-hit shutout against the

Cardinals that afternoon. He sent us home cold, sore, and very depressed.

★★★★

You ask, "If that was your worst day at a Cardinal game, what was your best?" It won't take long to think about that, but there are actually three thrilling days I will never forget.

The first was that day in 1955 when I got Stan Musial's autograph.

The second was the last game of the 1998 season. A day earlier Mark McGwire had hit home runs number 67 and 68 against Montreal. We had tickets for the Sunday afternoon finale when McGwire hit home runs numbers 69 and 70. It was a record we thought would never be broken.

And the third? Maybe the best of all. It was game three of the 2006 World Series in the brand new Busch Stadium. Mitch and I watched Chris Carpenter shut down the Detroit Tigers on three hits, winning 5–0. The Cardinals went on to win the series, four games to one.

Oh, and those baseball cards? In 2002 Mitch and I saw many of the cards I had owned in my personal collection. They were on display in souvenir shops all over Cooperstown. There was a 1952 Mantle card for sale at a price over $20,000. I had one of those cards and many others that would sell today at a very high price.

But that dream went up in smoke—literally. One spring break, when I came home from college, I found that Mom had done some closet cleaning. She had burned my entire baseball card collection in a metal drum in the backyard.

The family has teased her a lot for her mistake, but it makes little difference to me. They had their purpose at a moment in time, contributing to my incurable case of "Cardinal fever." Priceless!

10 WAYS TO KNOW YOU HAVE CARDINAL FEVER

You know you have Cardinal fever...if you name your pet dog Pujols.

You know you have Cardinal fever...if you and your neighborhood friends are known as the Gas House Gang.

You know you have Cardinal fever...if you celebrate each birthday with a hotdog at Busch Stadium.

You know you have Cardinal fever...if you think Red Schoendienst is the dean of the College of Cardinals.

You know you have Cardinal fever... if you invite Fredbird to go with you on your family vacation.

You know you have Cardinal fever... if you fly the Cardinal pennant on a flagpole at your house.

You know you have Cardinal fever... if you use "Herzog" as your password to get on the Internet.

You know you have Cardinal fever... if your favorite horse is a Clydesdale.

You know you have Cardinal fever... if you have ever tried to do an Ozzie Smith flip.

You know you have Cardinal fever... if you never had a doubt that St. Louis would win the 2006 World Series.